CCSS **Genre** Realistic Fiction

Essential Question
What can our connections to the world teach us?

Helping Out

by **Max Olsen**   illustrated by **James Stayte**

CHAPTER 1

After the Earthquake

When a massive earthquake struck the city of San José in Costa Rica, Curtis couldn't take his eyes off the TV screen. The news showed pictures of fallen buildings and people being carried out of the rubble on stretchers. Curtis wished he could help but wasn't sure what he could do.

On the way to school the following morning, he kept thinking about the disaster. Looking out the window on the bus, he wondered what it would be like if an earthquake hit his hometown. He was startled when a siren blared as an ambulance raced past.

At the start of class, Miss Johnston took attendance. Then the class talked about the earthquake, and Miss Johnston announced that she was recruiting volunteers to participate in a project to help the people in San José.

Curtis's hand shot up immediately. Suddenly it seemed as if there *could* be a way for him to help the earthquake victims, after all. Around him other students were volunteering, too, and soon Miss Johnston had counted six of them, including Curtis and his best friend, Chen.

"That's good," Miss Johnston said, "but remember, volunteering means giving up your own time to help others. We'll have a planning meeting for the project here at lunchtime, so be in the classroom right after the lunch bell, please."

Curtis caught Chen's eye.

"What do you think we can do to help?" he asked.

"I don't know," Chen replied. "They've been asking for donations on TV. Maybe we could raise money by getting paid to run errands for our neighbors."

"It might take quite a while to bring in enough money, though," Curtis said gently. He knew there must be something else they could do, but he couldn't think of any alternatives.

Chen wasn't worried. He was sure Miss Johnston and the other volunteers would have plenty of ideas.

When Curtis and Chen arrived at the meeting, Megan, Joella, Djamila, and Jorge were already sitting around the table. Miss Johnston explained that the students must decide what they were going to do to help the people in San José. It was going to be their own project.

"I was thinking about putting on a music concert," Jorge said, starting the discussion.

The group felt enthusiastic about the idea until Megan pointed out that only Chen and Jorge could play instruments. Joella added that they had to act quickly and organizing a concert would take time.

They brainstormed some more, bouncing their ideas across the table from one person to another. They considered collecting aluminum cans to exchange for cash, and someone even suggested getting their parents to drive to Costa Rica in cars loaded with supplies!

Curtis didn't propose anything. He was just happy to help with whatever the group chose, but he knew they needed to agree on something that excited everyone.

"Hey!" Jorge said, breaking into the discussion as he moved his wheelchair in closer to the table. "Miss Johnston told us that the people of San José need food and clean water, so that's what we should send them."

"He's right," Djamila agreed. "We should collect groceries and bottled water. My parents own the supermarket on Durham Street, and I know they'd be happy to donate lots of canned food."

"We could ask other stores in town for donations, too," Curtis added.

"My mom works at a factory where they make cereal," Megan added. "I bet they'd give us boxes of cereal."

Everyone voted that sending food to San José was the best idea, and soon the room was humming with excitement as the volunteers proposed ways to collect donations.

"Let's work in pairs and ask our parents to drive us around to different businesses," Chen suggested.

Chen hunted through the phone book to identify 30 key businesses to approach for donations. Then he divided the list into three and allocated ten businesses for each pair of students to visit.

Miss Johnston was clearly pleased with their work when she checked in later. "Well done, everyone. Let's meet again next Monday to sort the donated goods you've collected."

"Want to work with me?" Chen asked, turning to Curtis.

"Of course!" he replied. Then he had a thought, and he called out to everyone as they were leaving, "Wait! Shouldn't we figure out how we'll get the groceries to Costa Rica?"

"Good point," said Chen. "I remember seeing on the news last night that the Costa Rican Red Cross is working in the quake zone, so why doesn't one of us contact them?"

"Can you two be in charge of that? You could call or probably even e-mail them," Djamila said.

"Sure," Curtis replied. "No problem."

Curtis and Chen found the e-mail address for the Red Cross in Costa Rica on the Internet, and Curtis wrote to them asking for advice on how to send the supplies.

This was fun. There was something really exciting about having a connection with another country.

CHAPTER 2

Oh, No!

As soon as Curtis woke up on Saturday morning, his stomach began turning cartwheels. Although he was looking forward to collecting groceries, he was nervous, too. Would they be able to persuade business owners to donate?

As he rushed through his breakfast, he wondered what the people of San José were having for theirs. As soon as he had finished eating, Chen and his mom arrived to pick him up.

"Come on, Curtis, let's go!" Chen called.

His friend's eagerness made Curtis feel more confident, and as Chen's mom drove them to a fruit and vegetable stand on Main Street, Curtis began to feel more relaxed.

When Curtis and Chen hopped out of the car, Chen's mom called, "I'll be right here if you need me, but remember what Miss Johnston said—you need to make the decisions about your project."

The owner of the fruit and vegetable stand listened politely while Curtis carefully explained what he and Chen were collecting and why.

When he was done, the owner smiled and said, "I'd love to help out, but these vegetables wouldn't keep long enough for you to send them all the way to Costa Rica. By the time they got there, they'd be compost."

6

Curtis and Chen looked at each other in horror. Why hadn't they thought of that?

"Thank you anyway, sir," Curtis mumbled in embarrassment.

The next storekeeper congratulated the boys on their efforts, but explained that he'd already given money to the earthquake appeal and couldn't donate groceries as well. It was the same at the next two businesses.

"Maybe this wasn't such a good idea," Chen groaned. But then the woman at the mini-mart gave the boys five boxes of powdered milk and a bag of dried apricots, saying, "I've got relatives in Costa Rica. It's good to see people like you getting out and helping."

Curtis was relieved to finally get a donation, but he didn't feel as if they'd collected very much, especially when he saw Jorge and Djamila leaving her parents' supermarket with a shopping cart groaning under the weight of dozens of cans of vegetables and bottles of water!

By mid-afternoon the boys had visited their ten businesses and were feeling much happier. "We might not have collected as much as Djamila and Jorge," said Chen, "but we've practically filled the trunk of the car."

After Chen and his mom had dropped Curtis back home, he checked his e-mail, hoping for a reply from the Costa Rican Red Cross. Nothing was in his inbox, but he wasn't worried. They were probably just too busy to reply right away.

At school the next Monday, it took nearly an hour for the class to unload the donated groceries. Megan's mom had been given 50 boxes of cereal by her factory, and it took Joella's dad two trips to bring all their donated groceries to school. The pile at the back of the classroom was enormous—almost as tall as Curtis!

During recess, the team worked hard sorting the groceries, and when they had almost finished, Curtis hurried to the library to check his e-mail again. He was thrilled to see a message from *Cruz Roja Costarricense*.

Curtis didn't need to speak Spanish to know it came from the Costa Rican Red Cross. He opened the e-mail with great excitement, but the message hit him like a slap in the face. He felt sick with disappointment. What would he tell the others?

He printed out the e-mail and walked reluctantly back to the classroom.

The volunteers were too busy to notice that Curtis had returned, but when Miss Johnston looked up, she instantly recognized that something was seriously wrong.

"What is it, Curtis?" she asked, hurrying over to him.

"We can't send the food," he replied quietly, handing Miss Johnston the e-mail from the Costa Rican Red Cross.

Miss Johnston took the e-mail from him and read it quickly. "Bad news, everyone. Curtis got a reply from the Red Cross in Costa Rica, and we need to talk about what they've said," she said. Then she read the e-mail aloud.

Dear students,

Here at the Red Cross, we are touched that you want to help with the earthquake recovery effort in San José. It's wonderful that school students are trying to help the unfortunate people who have been affected by this disaster. Sadly, however, it is not practical to send groceries to the earthquake zone. This is because the cost of sending food would be more than its value, and in any case, with the current situation in San José, we have no way of transporting it to where it is needed.

There was a murmur of disappointment around the classroom as the implications of the message sank in.

Miss Johnston continued reading,

What we desperately need are donations of money so that we can buy essential supplies in Costa Rica close to the area that is most affected. From there it will be easier to deliver the supplies to the people who need them. Thank you again for your kind efforts, and I hope you will consider making a donation of money to the Costa Rican Red Cross.

The e-mail was from Maria Zaragoza, Relief Manager, Cruz Roja Costarricense.

Djamila had started to cry, but everyone else was silent. It seemed as if all their hard work had been for nothing.

"What can we do?" asked Megan.

"There's nothing we can do but take all the groceries back to the businesses that donated them," answered Joella.

Curtis was about to agree when a thought came to him.

"Wait!" he said. "We don't have to take the groceries back. I've got a better idea."

CHAPTER 3

Market Day

The expression on Curtis's face had changed from terrible disappointment to great excitement, and everyone was looking at him expectantly.

Pointing at the cartons of groceries, he said, "If the Red Cross needs money, we can simply sell this food and raise money that way."

"That's a great idea!" said Jorge. "We can transform the groceries into cash!"

Miss Johnston remained silent, but she was listening carefully to what the volunteers were saying.

"But where can we sell everything?" Joella asked, looking doubtful.

"At the Saturday market where my gran sells her knitting every week," Curtis responded, explaining that anyone could set up a stall there.

Suddenly it seemed to Curtis that he had all the answers at his fingertips. He and Chen hadn't managed to collect as many groceries as the others, but he knew he had made an important contribution by finding the perfect solution to their problem.

Miss Johnston joined in the discussion at last. "I believe Curtis's idea might just work, but before we can sell anything at the market, we will have to ask for permission from all the businesses that donated groceries."

"You know what this means?" Chen cried. "Now that we aren't sending the food all the way to Costa Rica, we can go back to the fruit and vegetable stall and to the butcher and ask them to donate their produce to raise money for San José. What do you think, Curtis?"

"That's a really good idea," Curtis agreed.

The more people looked to him for his opinion, the more confident he felt about giving it. He took a deep breath and said, "We should work in pairs again so that we can prepare everything in time for the market. Djamila and Jorge, can you two arrange for us to rent a stall at the market?" Djamila and Jorge nodded.

"Megan and Joella," Curtis continued, "would you create a sign for the stall? People need to know their money is going to a charitable cause. Chen, you and I should revisit some of the stores we went to on Saturday and ask for donations of fresh food, and we should all call the businesses that have already given us donations and make sure it's okay for us to sell what they gave us."

Curtis was incredibly happy now that he knew the volunteers *could* make a real difference in San José ... and it was his own idea that had made it possible. He was convinced the stall would be a success. People would be sure to buy the groceries when they saw that the money was going to support the earthquake appeal.

That Friday evening, Curtis loaded the cabbages and bananas that they'd been given to sell into his dad's car and wrote himself a reminder note to take the meat from the refrigerator in the morning. Then he set his alarm for six in the morning so he'd be up early enough to organize everything before the market opened.

When he arrived at the market, Miss Johnston, Djamila, and Jorge were already there. As the other students arrived with their boxes of groceries, the stall began to take shape.

"Looking good!" the market manager said in approval as she passed by. "You must have the biggest stall here."

Curtis, who was proudly gazing at the massive sign hanging from their table, asked her what she thought of it.

"ALL PROCEEDS TO THE RED CROSS COSTA RICA," the manager read aloud. "Oh, that will really grab people's attention," she said with a nod.

Minutes later shoppers began gathering around the stall and the groceries started to sell.

Suddenly something extraordinary began to happen. Instead of paying the prices the students were asking, people offered much more.

"I'll take a can of beans, please," a young man with a baby in a backpack said, pointing to the pile of cans in front of Curtis. He handed over a 20-dollar bill in payment, and when Curtis tried to give him his change, the man told him not to bother.

"Keep it," he said. "The people in San José need it more than I do."

To Curtis's amazement and delight, the same thing happened repeatedly with other buyers, and later in the morning, things got even better.

A woman said apologetically to Curtis that she didn't want to buy anything, but could she just make a contribution?

"No problem!" Curtis said with a grin. "I mean, thank you very much."

At the end of the day when the students helped Miss Johnston count up their earnings, the total was more than Curtis could ever have imagined.

"What have we learned?" Miss Johnston asked before everyone headed home.

"We should always ask organizations what they need before trying to help," Chen answered.

Chen was right, but Curtis knew that he had learned something equally important. He had learned that everyone can help out—it's just a matter of finding the right way to do it.

Respond to Reading

Summarize

Use key details from *Helping Out* to summarize the story. Your graphic organizer may help you.

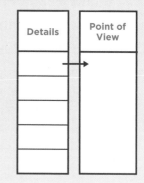

Details	Point of View

Text Evidence

1. How can you tell that *Helping Out* is realistic fiction? Give examples from the text to support your answer. **GENRE**

2. Is this story told by a first-person or third-person narrator? Use details from the story to describe the narrator's point of view. **POINT OF VIEW**

3. On page 4, the author says the room was "humming with excitement." Find another example of personification on page 6. How do these examples add to the story? **PERSONIFICATION**

4. Write about how the events on pages 9 through 12 would change if they were described by Curtis as a first-person narrator. Use details from the story in your answer. **WRITE ABOUT READING**

Compare Texts

Read a poem about a girl who connects to a different time and place by interviewing her grandmother.

— A — Journalistic Journey

Interview a senior citizen
about their time at school?
What a project, Miss Roberts!
Who can Laura ask?
Laura is running,
running home from school,
racing, chasing
through the bracing wind.
Then the idea,
leaping into sight
like Bonnie the cat
through the window in the morning.

"Grandma, Grandma!
Tell me about school,
back when you were young
in Costa Rica."
Questions and answers,
teachers and school dances—
a life that Laura is
never going to see.
It's buried in time,
but Laura is a miner,
digging deeper into history,
question by question.

"What an interview!"
Grandma sounds impressed.
"You're better than reporters on TV."
Could it be true?
And now Laura is dreaming,
captured by her future:
a super interviewer
on a journalistic journey.
An article on Grandma—
is this her first assignment
as a reporter employed
by Troydon School?

Make Connections

What does Laura in *A Journalistic Journey* learn about herself as she makes connections with a different place and time? **ESSENTIAL QUESTION**

How is what Curtis learns similar to what Laura learns? How are their discoveries different?
TEXT TO TEXT

Focus on Literary Elements

Imagery Poets and other writers use imagery to make their writing richer and to give readers a stronger sense of the ideas they are writing about. Imagery can include the use of metaphor and simile, or it can simply use vivid descriptive words. Imagery often uses the senses (touch, sight, hearing, smell, taste) to help readers form mental images of what is being described.

Read and Find In *A Journalistic Journey*, the imagery in the first verse (page 17) includes a simile that describes how Laura's idea arrives in her mind with a movement "like Bonnie the cat."

In the next verse (page 18), the writer uses the metaphor of mining and vivid language to describe the way Laura questions her grandmother for more and more information.

Your Turn

Close your eyes and imagine a person or scene from your early childhood. It could be meeting a relative, attending a special festival, or visiting a new place. Imagine this with all of your senses: What can you see, hear, smell, taste, and feel? Then jot down words or phrases about what you saw, heard, smelled, tasted, and touched. Use these notes to help you write a poem or short story that includes the person or scene you imagined. Illustrate your writing and share your finished work with your group.